# Nelson Grammar

# Pupil Book 6

OXFORD

UNIVERSITY PRESS

# OXFORD
## UNIVERSITY PRESS

Great Clarendon Street, Oxford, OX2 6DP, United Kingdom

Oxford University Press is a department of the University of Oxford.
It furthers the University's objective of excellence in research, scholarship,
and education by publishing worldwide. Oxford is a registered trade mark
of Oxford University Press in the UK and in certain other countries

British Library Cataloguing in Publication Data

Data available

ISBN: 978-1-4085-2393-3

3 5 7 9 10 8 6 4

Paper used in the production of this book is a natural, recyclable product made from
wood grown in sustainable forests. The manufacturing process conforms to the
environmental regulations of the country of origin.

Printed in China by Imago

**Acknowledgements**

Series editor: John Jackman
Cover illustrations: Tony Forbes
Page make-up: OKS Prepress, India

**Oxford OWL** Discover eBooks, inspirational
resources, advice and support
**www.oxfordowl.co.uk**

# Contents

|  | Scope and sequence | 4 |
|---|---|---|
| Unit 1 | Sentences | 6 |
| Unit 2 | Sentences | 8 |
| Unit 3 | Homophones and homonyms | 10 |
| Unit 4 | Pronouns | 12 |
| Unit 5 | Verbs | 14 |
| Unit 6 | Sentences | 16 |
| Unit 7 | Verbs | 18 |
| Unit 8 | Sentences | 20 |
| Unit 9 | Confusing words | 22 |
| Unit 10 | Sentences | 24 |
| Unit 11 | Improving writing | 26 |
| Unit 12 | Nouns | 28 |
| Unit 13 | Improving writing | 30 |
| Unit 14 | Confusing words | 32 |
| Unit 15 | Punctuation | 34 |
| Unit 16 | Sentences | 36 |
| Unit 17 | Verbs | 38 |
| Unit 18 | Verbs | 40 |
| Unit 19 | Standard and Non-standard English | 42 |
| Unit 20 | Sentences | 44 |
| Unit 21 | Punctuation | 46 |
| Unit 22 | Paragraphs | 48 |
| Unit 23 | Verbs | 50 |
| Unit 24 | Standard English | 52 |
| Unit 25 | Punctuation | 54 |
| Unit 26 | Sentences | 56 |
| Unit 27 | Verbs | 58 |
| Unit 28 | Standard English | 60 |
|  | How to use this book | 62 |

# Book 6 Scope and Sequence

| Unit | Pupil Book | Pupil Book Focus | Pupil Book Practice | Pupil Book Extension | Resource Book Support | Resource Book Extension |
|---|---|---|---|---|---|---|
| 1 | **sentences**: subject and object | identifying the subject and object in given sentences | completing sentences with interesting objects | adding adjectives to subjects and objects to make interesting sentences/constructing sentences from given subject–object pairs | identifying subjects and objects in sentences/completing chart/writing sentences with given subjects | making given nouns the subject, then the object of own sentences |
| 2 | **sentences**: subject and predicate | identifying subjects and predicates in sentences | matching subjects and predicates to form sentences | writing interesting subjects to complete sentences/writing interesting predicates to complete sentences | identifying subject and predicate in sentences/completing sentences with interesting predicates | using given nouns as both subject and predicate in pairs of sentences |
| 3 | **homophones and homonyms** | completing sentences with correct homophone/identifying parts of speech – homonyms | solving clues with correct homophone – homonym/sentence writing | using unusual homophones in sentences | choosing the correct homophone/identifying parts of speech – homonyms/sentence writing | writing homophones for given words/using pairs of homonyms in sentences |
| 4 | **pronouns**: relative | completing sentence with relative pronouns | joining pairs of sentences with relative pronouns | completing sentences with *whose* and *whom* | joining pairs of sentences with relative pronouns/completing sentences with *whose* and *whom* | writing sentences with relative pronouns about given subjects |
| 5 | **verbs**: modals | identifying modal verbs in sentences | completing sentences with *may – can*; *might – must*; *could – would – should* | writing sentences with given modal verbs | using *could – would – should* in own writing/writing sentences with given modal verbs | using modal verbs in given scenarios |
| 6 | **sentences**: relative clauses | identifying relative clause and associated noun in sentences | completing sentences with *who* or *which* | adding relative clauses to main clauses/adding main clauses to relative clauses | completing sentences with relative clauses/writing description using relative clauses | positioning relative clauses to make sense |
| 7 | **verbs**: round-up | putting given verbs into a variety of tenses | changing sentences into a variety of other tenses | writing sentences with past simple and past perfect tenses | changing sentences into given tenses | writing sentences with given tenses about given subjects |
| 8 | **sentences**: single- and multi-clause | identifying main clauses and conjunctions in sentences | joining pairs of sentences with co-ordinating conjunctions | adding conjunctions and main clauses to given main clauses | identifying main clauses and conjunctions in sentences/joining pairs of sentences to make multi-clause sentences | writing single-clause sentences with given phrases/turning single-clause sentences into multi-clause sentences |
| 9 | **confusing words** | correcting mistakes in sentences using *all together – altogether*; *lie – lay*; *past – passed* | completing sentences with *all together – altogether*, *lie – lay*; *past – passed* | completing sentences with verb *to lie* | completing sentences with *all together – altogether*; *lie – lay*; *past – passed*/sentence writing with verb *to lie* | sentence writing with more unusual confusing words |
| 10 | **sentences**: single- and multi-clause | identifying main and subordinate clauses in sentences | joining pairs of sentences with subordinating conjunctions | adding subordinate clauses to main clauses | identifying subordinate clauses/joining single-clause sentences to make multi-clause sentences | writing single-clause sentences with given phrases/turning sentences into multi-clause sentences |
| 11 | **improving writing**: vocabulary and detail | replacing overused words in sentences | expanding simple sentences/rewriting sentences to avoid repetition | improving sentences with vocabulary and detail | rewriting simple passage to improve vocabulary | rewriting sentences to avoid beginning with *I* |
| 12 | **nouns**: phrases | identifying noun phrases in sentences/forming noun phrases | identifying and expanding noun phrases | identifying noun phrases with infinitives/sentence writing with given noun phrases | identifying noun phrases in sentences/expanding noun phrases and using them in sentences | completing sentences with noun phrases as indicated/writing sentences with given infinitives |
| 13 | **improving writing**: presenting information | answering questions about structure of extended writing | completing a chart from given information | researching and presenting information | using information given in continuous prose about *Henry VIII's wives* to create a chart | researching information about the *Solar System* and creating a chart |
| 14 | **confusing words** | correcting mistakes in sentences | completing sentences with *who's* or *whose* | writing sentences with pairs of often confused words | choosing correct word to complete sentences | completing traditional poem/writing sentences |
| 15 | **punctuation**: hyphens in compound words | adding hyphens where appropriate | adding hyphens where appropriate | correcting ambiguous headlines with hyphens | contracting phrases into compound adjectives/writing numbers and fractions as words/making hyphenated and non-hyphenated compound words from given root words | explaining meaning of hyphenated and non-hyphenated phrases/contracting phrases into hyphenated compound adjectives |

\* denotes content that is not specified in the National Curriculum for England (2014) but which will support children's wider knowledge and understanding of grammar.

| Unit | Pupil Book | Pupil Book Focus | Pupil Book Practice | Pupil Book Extension | Resource Book Support | Resource Book Extension |
|------|-----------|------------------|---------------------|----------------------|----------------------|------------------------|
| 16 | **sentences**: direct speech round-up* | punctuating direct speech sentences/setting out as conversation | completing and punctuating direct speech sentences | writing conversation in direct and indirect speech | writing a conversation with speech marks from speech bubbles | writing a conversation from picture stimulus |
| 17 | **verbs**: modal/auxiliary verbs* | identifying auxiliary verbs | completing sentences with *must – ought to/ have to, has to* or *had better* | writing sentences with modal and auxiliary verbs | ranking statements with auxiliary verbs in order of strength of purpose/ sentence writing with auxiliary verbs | writing a conversation about a given situation to include auxiliary verbs |
| 18 | **verbs**: active and passive | identifying active and passive verbs in sentences | changing sentences from active to passive/ passive to active | writing active sentences with given verbs/ changing sentences to passive | identifying active and passive verbs in sentences/changing active sentences to passive sentences | completing sentences with active and passive verbs/ writing active and passive sentences with given verbs |
| 19 | **Standard English**: slang | identifying how Non-standard English sentences would be written in Standard English | changing words into Standard English in sentences | interpreting Cockney rhyming slang | changing slang words and phrases in sentences to Standard English/ rewriting sentences in Standard English/ interpreting Cockney rhyming slang | rewriting a slang conversation in Standard English |
| 20 | **sentences**: conditional clauses* | identifying conditional clauses in sentences | completing sentences with conditional clauses | completing sentences with frontal conditional clauses | completing sentences with conditional clauses/ writing about the weekend including conditional clauses | writing sentences with given conditional conjunctions |
| 21 | **punctuation**: semicolon and colon | explaining use of semicolon and colon in sentences | punctuating sentences | writing sentences about given topics with semicolons, colons and dashes | adding missing semicolons and colons to sentences/ writing sentences with semicolons and colons | constructing sentences from given situations using semicolons and colons |
| 22 | **paragraphs**: discursive writing | answering questions about structure in extended writing | supported writing for a discursive piece on given subject | writing a discursive piece on choice of subject | writing discursive piece with given paragraph plan and arguments | researching and writing discursive piece |
| 23 | **verbs**: active and passive | identifying active and passive verbs in sentences | completing passive sentences with agents/ with actions | writing active and passive sentences from given pairs of subjects and objects | identifying active and passive sentences/ changing active sentences to passive sentences | completing sentences with active and passive verbs/ writing active and passive sentences with given verbs/supplying agents for passive sentences |
| 24 | **Standard English**: grammatical constructions | changing Non-standard English sentences into Standard English | choosing correct word to complete sentences/ rewriting sentences in Standard English | writing Non-standard English conversation/ changing it to Standard English | identifying Non-standard words and phrases in sentences/correcting Non-standard English in sentences/rewriting double negative sentences | correcting Non-standard English sentences/writing sentences in Standard English |
| 25 | **punctuation**: hyphens with prefixes | adding hyphens | writing hyphenated words with given prefixes/using hyphenated words in sentences | writing sentences with *re* words unhyphenated and hyphenated | identify and correcting words needing a hyphen/matching hyphenated words to correct definition/ sentence writing | sentence writing with hyphenated/non-hyphenated words |
| 26 | **sentences**: clause round-up* | identifying main clauses in sentences | completing sentences with given type of clause | extending sentences with adverb, relative and conditional clauses | writing story opening from picture stimulus and given clauses | writing story opening from picture stimulus to include given clauses |
| 27 | **verbs**: active/passive/subjunctives | identifying subjunctive verbs in sentences | rewriting active sentences as passive sentences/rewriting sentences to use the subjunctive form | changing informal sentences into formal sentences using the subjunctive *were* | writing active and passive sentences for each pair of nouns | forming the subjunctive from infinitives/writing sentences with subjunctives from word equations |
| 28 | **Standard English**: vocabulary | discussing different forms of writing for different purposes and audiences | translating and writing text messages/ translating and writing emails/identifying formal English expressions in letter | writing text message, email and letter on chosen subject | rewriting a Non-standard English email for a non-native speaker | creating a Non-standard English email to a classmate/correcting an email |

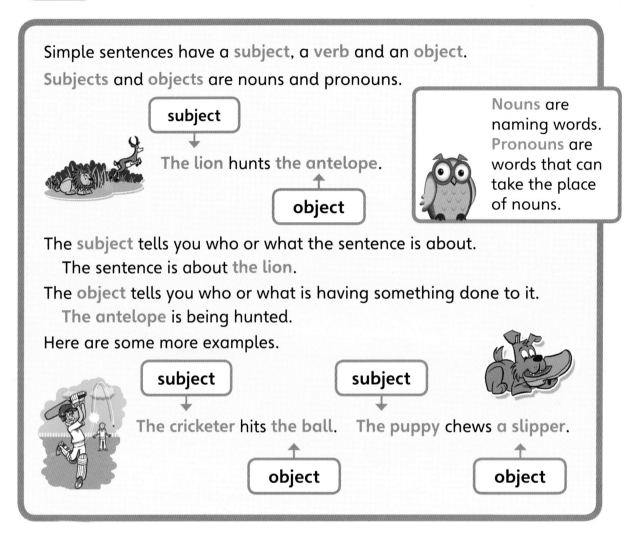

Simple sentences have a subject, a verb and an object.

Subjects and objects are nouns and pronouns.

**subject**

The lion hunts the antelope.

**object**

Nouns are naming words. Pronouns are words that can take the place of nouns.

The subject tells you who or what the sentence is about.
The sentence is about the lion.

The object tells you who or what is having something done to it.
The antelope is being hunted.

Here are some more examples.

**subject**          **subject**

The cricketer hits the ball.   The puppy chews a slipper.

**object**            **object**

## Focus

**A** What is the *subject* of each sentence?

1 Sam concentrated on his reading.

2 The horse jumped the fence.

3 The archers shot at the targets.

4 Nina ate a biscuit.

**B** What is the *object* in each sentence?

1 Ali washed the car.

2 My friends bought me a present.

3 Policemen catch robbers.

4 The spider devoured the fly.

## Practice

Copy and finish each sentence by adding an interesting *object* to each one.

**1** Kali grabbed _____ .

**2** The young girl spilt _____ .

**3** Frank bought some _____ .

**4** The giraffe ate _____ .

**5** My cousin made _____ .

## Extension

**A** Copy the sentences into your book.
Make each one more interesting by adding an *adjective*
in front of each *subject* and each *object*.

**1** The man ate the pie.

**2** The decorator painted the wall.

**3** The boy flew his kite.

**4** The cobra hissed at the woman.

**5** Blackbirds eat worms.

**B** Write sentences of your own using
these pairs of *subjects* and *objects*.

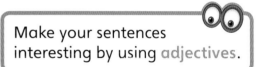

Make your sentences
interesting by using adjectives.

| subject | object |
| --- | --- |
| **1** cat | tree |
| **2** pirate | treasure |
| **3** musician | song |
| **4** bird | nest |
| **5** policewoman | traffic |

# Sentences

A sentence has two parts.
The subject is the person or thing that the sentence is about.
The predicate is the rest of the sentence.

| subject | predicate |
|---------|-----------|
| My family | is very large. |
| The dog | barked at the stranger. |
| Everyone | cheered loudly. |

To find the subject of a sentence, first find the verb.

The dog barked at the stranger.

Ask who or what barked in the sentence: the dog
The subject is The dog.
This is a very simple sentence that does not tell us very much.
It is not very interesting!
We can make the sentence more interesting by adding to the subject.

subject ↓          predicate ↓

The fierce, angry dog barked at the stranger.

We can make the sentence even more
interesting by adding to the predicate.

We add adjectives to make the subject more interesting.

subject ↓          predicate ↓

The fierce, angry dog barked at the mysterious stranger.

**Focus**

**A** What is the *subject* of each sentence?

1 That valuable book has been left in the rain!
2 A flock of geese frightened the children.
3 The enthusiastic audience clapped wildly.

**B** What is the *predicate* in each sentence?

1 The mist lingered in the bottom of the valley.
2 Every old car causes pollution.
3 The gigantic tree had fallen across the road.

## Practice

Join each *subject* with the correct *predicate* to make a sentence.

| Subject | Predicate |
|---|---|
| **1** An octopus | went all the way around the building. |
| **2** The tennis player | don't like flying. |
| **3** The queue | is coming to visit. |
| **4** My aunt | has eight legs. |
| **5** Some people | served an ace. |

## Extension

**A** Add an interesting *subject* to each *predicate*.

**1** _____ swayed dangerously in the wind.

**2** _____ crept through the undergrowth.

**3** _____ cast magic spells.

**4** _____ burst through the clouds.

**5** _____ journeyed in space.

**B** Add an interesting *predicate* to each *subject*.

**1** The firework display _____.

**2** Many athletes _____.

**3** The red squirrel _____.

**4** Ancient monuments _____.

**5** The weird sculpture _____.

# Homophones and homonyms

**Homophones** are words that sound the same BUT they:

* are spelled differently
* have a different meaning.

Using the wrong **homophone** can make what we write ridiculous!

He made a sandcastle on the **beech**.
What the writer means is:   He made a sandcastle on the **beach**.

**Homonyms** are words that are **different parts of speech** BUT they:

* sound the same
* are spelled the same.

We watched the **play**.     They **play** musical instruments.

noun            verb

**Focus**

**A**  Choose the correct *homophone* from the brackets to complete each sentence.

**1** The cowboy _____ into town.        (*rode/road*)

**2** The _____ approached the castle.   (*night/knight*)

**3** I _____ what I had to do.           (*new/knew*)

**B**  Say if the italic word in each sentence is used as a *noun* or a *verb*.

**1  a** I have to *type* this letter again!
   **b** What *type* of butterfly is that?

**2  a** Put the fruit in the *bowl*.
   **b** I *bowl* left-handed.

**3  a** *Book* the tickets before they all go.
   **b** A *book* of raffle tickets costs a pound.

## Practice

**A** Solve the clues with the correct *homophone*.

1 material obtained from trees     (*would/wood*)

2 a type of fish     (*plaice/place*)

3 opposite of left     (*write/right*)

4 to pull along behind     (*toe/tow*)

5 a facial feature     (*nose/knows*)

**B** Write clues for the *homophones* that were NOT the answers in **A**.

**C** The answer to each pair of clues is a *homonym*. Write the *homonym*.

1 **a** very serious     **b** where people are buried

2 **a** outer part of a tree     **b** noise a dog makes

3 **a** move back and forwards     **b** large stone

4 **a** where ships unload cargo     **b** a type of drink

5 **a** to let something go     **b** does not cost anything

**D** Choose a *homonym* for two of the clues in **C**.

Write two sentences for each *homonym* showing you understand the different meanings.

Use a dictionary to help you.

## Extension

These pairs of *homophones* are more unusual.

Use each of them in a sentence of your own to show you clearly understand the meaning.

1 chord/cord     2 coin/quoin

3 flow/floe     4 queue/cue

5 sight/cite     6 wrote/rote

A **pronoun** takes the place of a **noun**.

**The doctor** examined the patient.

**She** examined the patient.

The following pronouns are called **relative pronouns**.

| who | whom | whose | which | that |

**Relative pronouns** are special because they do two jobs.

**1** They take the place of **nouns**.

**2** They act as **conjunctions**, and they are **related** to the **noun** that comes before them in a sentence.

We have a cousin.

He lives in America.

We have a cousin **who** lives in America.

> **Conjunctions** are joining words.

The artist painted a picture.

The picture won a prize.

The artist painted a picture **which** won a prize.

**Who** is used for people. **Which**/**That** are used for animals and things.

---

**Focus**

Copy the sentences.
Use the *relative pronoun who* or *which* to complete each one.

**1** She was on the bus _____ broke down.

**2** I mowed the grass _____ had grown very tall.

**3** We listened to the street musicians _____ played outside the town hall.

**4** She likes poetry _____ tells a story.

**5** The photographer, _____ takes wildlife pictures, is very talented.

Copy and join each pair of sentences using *who*, *which* or *that*.

1 Mary blew out the candles. The candles were on her cake.
2 The explorer found an island. The island was uninhabited.
3 Giraffes have long necks. Long necks enable them
   to feed from high branches.
4 This book is about astronauts. Astronauts landed on the Moon.
5 The drawbridge crossed the moat. The moat went
   around the castle.

## Extension

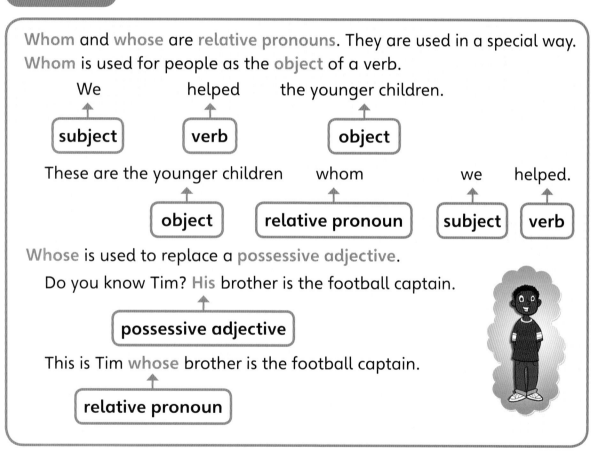

Copy and complete each sentence with *whom* or *whose*.

1 Could you tell me to _____ I should complain?
2 I think I know _____ these shoes are.
3 _____ parents are coming to the play?
4 This is my sister _____ I think you have met.

Sometimes verbs are made up of more than one word.

These verbs are made up of auxiliary or helper verbs + main verb.
This group of auxiliary verbs is very useful.

| may | might | could |
|-----|-------|-------|
| can | must | would |
|     |       | should |

These are called modal verbs.

**can** and **may**:

> She **can** recite her 12 times table.
> **May** I recite my 12 times table to you?

**might** and **must**:

> You **must** learn your 12 times table.
> I **might** ask Dad to help me.

**could**, **would** and **should**:

> I **could** practise every day.
> I **would** like to get them all right.
> I **should** spend more time learning them.

**Focus**

What is the *modal verb* in each sentence?

1  I must remember to take my homework to school.
2  I should warn you that the weather will get worse.
3  It might be a good idea to ring up and check what time it starts.
4  Can you reach the top shelf?
5  They would like to visit in the spring.
6  I could eat a horse!
7  You may leave at six o'clock.
8  May I borrow that CD?

**A** Copy and complete the sentences with *can* or *may*.

1 _____ I have a cup of tea and a slice of toast?

2 _____ you find your way?

3 You _____ go to the library if you _____ find your library card.

**B** Copy and complete the sentences with *might* or *must*.

1 If you _____ sing along, do it quietly!

2 The river _____ flood if it keeps on raining.

3 She _____ set off now because the bus _____ be early.

**C** Copy and complete the sentences with *could*, *would* or *should*.

1 We _____ easily climb that mountain.

2 We _____ not attempt to climb that mountain.

3 We _____ be foolish to climb that mountain.

Write sentences using these pairs of verbs.
Underline the *modal verb* in each sentence.

1 **a** can go                    **b** may go

2 **a** might arrive              **b** must arrive

3 **a** would remember            **b** could remember

4 **a** should leave              **b** could leave

# Sentences

Another name for a relative clause is an adjective clause.

To make sentences more interesting, we can use relative clauses.

A relative clause:

• begins with a relative pronoun:

who   whom   whose   which   that

• tells us more about a noun or pronoun in the main clause.

main clause       = Grandad had some stamps
relative clause  = which were very valuable.

Grandad had some stamps which were very valuable.

main clause       = The audience applauded the actor
relative clause  = who had given a wonderful performance.

The audience applauded the actor who had given a wonderful performance.

We use who when we are writing about a person.
I helped the boy who had fallen off his bicycle.

We use which/that when we are writing about an animal or thing.
Will you hang out the towels which have been washed?
This is the jigsaw piece that completes the puzzle.

## Focus

Copy the sentences.
Underline the *relative clause* in each sentence.
Put a ring around the noun it tells us about.

1 Where is the sock that matches this one?
2 I received a postcard from my sister who is on holiday in Greece.
3 She watered the plant that had drooping leaves.
4 May I speak to the person who left this message?
5 The farmer made a scarecrow that frightened the birds.

Copy and complete the sentences with *who* or *which*.

**1** I found an old coin _____ had been buried for hundreds of years.

**2** These people, _____ use the well, live in the village.

**3** Is Saturn the planet _____ has the rings around it?

**4** The plane, _____ flew faster than the speed of sound, was called Concorde.

**5** I know the people _____ have moved in next door.

## Extension

**A** Copy and complete each sentence by adding a *relative clause* to the main clause to make interesting sentences.

   **1** They found the bag _____.

   **2** Do you know the fairy tale _____?

   **3** The police caught the robber _____.

   **4** We saw the film _____.

**B** Copy and complete each sentence by adding a *main clause* to the relative clause to make interesting sentences.

   **1** _____ who works in the garage.

   **2** _____ which the dog had buried.

   **3** _____ that the postman delivered.

   **4** _____ who sells fruit and vegetables.

17

# Verbs

Verbs tell us what happens, has happened or will happen.

The tense of a verb tells us when something happens – in the past, the present or the future.

- past simple tense      It snowed.
- past progressive tense      It was snowing.
- perfect tense      It has snowed.
- past perfect tense      It had snowed.
- present simple tense      It snows.
- present progressive tense      It is snowing.
- future tense      It will snow.

This is a round-up of the verb tenses you know.

## Focus

**A** Say the verb *tenses* with *It* for each verb.

| past simple | past progressive | perfect | past perfect |
|---|---|---|---|
| present simple | present progressive | future | |

**1** to rain      **2** to blow      **3** to hail      **4** to shine      **5** to drizzle

**B** Identify the *verb* in each sentence and say which *tense* it is.
     **1** The wind had gusted at 40kph.
     **2** The hail is battering the windows.
     **3** The fog swirled across the moors.
     **4** The lightning has struck the oak tree.
     **5** It will snow tomorrow.

**A** Write these sentences in the *present progressive tense* and the *past progressive tense*.

   **1** I shelter under a tree.

   **2** The thunder rumbles in the distance.

   **3** Flags flutter in the breeze.

**B** Write these sentences in the *perfect tense* and the *past perfect tense*.

   **1** The wind blows strongly.

   **2** The sun is shining brightly.

   **3** The clouds are obscuring the sun.

**C** Write these sentences in the *present simple tense* and the *past simple tense*.

   **1** It will rain.

   **2** The wind will blow.

   **3** It will drizzle.

**Extension**

Write a sentence using each pair of verbs.
Use the *past simple tense* and the *past perfect tense*.

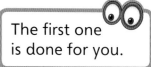
The first one is done for you.

| | Action I | Action 2 |
|---|---|---|
| **1** | to eat | to wash |

*I ate my lunch after I had washed my hands.*

| | | |
|---|---|---|
| **2** | to burn | to build |
| **3** | to borrow | to lose |
| **4** | to post | to write |

# Sentences

This is sometimes known as a simple sentence.

A sentence can sometimes be made up of **one main clause**. This is called a **single-clause** sentence.

> The hawk soared in the sky.

A sentence can also be made up of two or more main clauses joined by co-ordinating conjunctions:

This is sometimes known as a compound sentence.

| and | but | or |

This is a **multi-clause sentence**.

| main clause | The hawk soared in the sky. |
| main clause | We watched it disappear in the distance. |
| **multi-clause sentence** | The hawk soared in the sky **and** we watched it disappear in the distance. |
| main clause | We were caught in a traffic jam. |
| main clause | We made it on time. |
| **multi-clause sentence** | We were caught in a traffic jam **but** we made it on time. |
| main clause | It might rain tomorrow. |
| main clause | It might be fine. |
| **multi-clause sentence** | It might rain tomorrow **or** it might be fine. |

## Focus

Copy these multi-clause sentences.
Underline the *two main clauses* in each sentence and circle the *conjunction*.

1 The famous explorer went to Africa and she stayed there for many months.
2 The volcano erupted and lava poured down its sides.
3 I enjoy basketball but I'm too tired to play it now.
4 Are you going shopping today or will you wait until tomorrow?
5 It's my birthday tomorrow but I'm not having a party.

Use a *co-ordinating conjunction* to make a multi-clause sentence.

The conjunctions you can use are and, but and or.

| main clause | main clause |
|---|---|
| **1** My sandal is broken. | I think I can mend it. |
| **2** The library was busy. | There was nowhere to sit. |
| **3** I might have pizza for lunch. | I might have soup. |
| **4** I like this poem. | I don't like that one. |
| **5** The bird's feathers were blue. | Its beak was yellow. |
| **6** The castle was ancient. | Its walls were in ruins. |

## Extension

Add a *conjunction* and a *main clause* to each of these simple sentences to make a *multi-clause sentence*.

**1** The diver was looking for pearls _____.

**2** My head is aching _____.

**3** The factory is closing down _____.

**4** I might go for a swim _____.

**5** I may have misjudged you _____.

**6** We are a small community _____.

The conjunctions you can use are and, but and or.

**7** Is this sufficient _____.

**8** The restaurant was very good _____.

# Confusing words

Some words are very confusing!

- **all together and altogether**

  all together = collectively/as a group

  > Let's sing all together.

  altogether = all things considered/completely

  > Altogether, Sam is the better football player.
  > Altogether, the bill came to £25.

- **lay and lie**

  lay = put *something* in a horizontal position

  > Will you lay the table for dinner?

  lie = to put *yourself* in a horizontal position/to speak an untruth

  > I think I will lie down.
  > Did you lie to me?

- **past and passed**

  past = adjective / noun / adverb / preposition

  | | |
  |---|---|
  | adjective | This past year has been amazing. |
  | noun | I am interested in the past. |
  | adverb | Amy raced past. |
  | preposition | Amy raced past her friends. |

  passed = simple past tense of *to pass*

  > He passed the potatoes to me.

## Focus

Discuss and correct the *mistake* in each sentence.

1 We must walk to the library altogether.
2 The cars zoomed passed.
3 Lay down and have a rest.
4 Lie those sheets flat.
5 I am all together sure I am right.
6 In the passed, people travelled by horse and carriage.
7 He past by unnoticed.

## Practice

**A** The writer has confused *all together* and *altogether*.
Copy and correct the sentences.

**1** It's all together a bit of a mess!

**2** Let's go altogether.

**3** All together, it is a difficult problem.

**B** The writer has confused *lay* and *lie*.
Copy and correct the sentences.

**1** He lays down for a 10-minute nap every day.

**2** Are you lying the table?

**3** Why are you laying down?

**C** The writer has confused *past* and *passed*.
Copy and correct the sentences.

**1** The dog ran passed me.

**2** In the passed, I have visited Australia.

**3** The tiger strolled passed the water hole.

## Extension

The verb to lie (to move into a horizontal position) is tricky.

| Verb family name | Present tenses | Past tenses |
| --- | --- | --- |
| to lie | I lie | I lay |
| | I am lying | I have lain |
| | | I had lain |

Copy and complete each sentence with the *correct part of the verb*.

**1** Last night, I _____ on the sofa.

**2** I am _____ down for a little while.

**3** I had _____ awake all last night.

**4** He has _____ in bed all day!

# Sentences

These are sometimes known as compound sentences.

A sentence can be made up of one main clause.

   The election was held on Thursday.

Some multi-clause sentences use co-ordinating conjunctions to join two main clauses together.

   and         but         or

   The election was held on Thursday.

   The result was announced on Friday.

   The election was held on Thursday and the result was announced on Friday.

Some multi-clause sentences use subordinating conjunctions. These conjunctions introduce a clause which is less important than the main clause.

   There is one main clause.

   There are one or more subordinate clauses.

   Here are some useful subordinating conjunctions.

Subordinate means less important.

| Conjunctions | | | Pronouns |
|---|---|---|---|
| before | where | unless | who |
| until | because | so | which |
| although | while | as | that |
| wherever | even though | after | whose |
| when | if | | |

| main clause | subordinate clause |
|---|---|

The house had been empty for many years   before we bought it.

## Focus

In these sentences identify:
- the *main clause*
- the *subordinate clause*

1 The guitar was broken before I borrowed it.

2 Although it was very steep, we climbed the mountain.

3 My sister will come over when she has finished her work.

4 The people next door have a noisy dog which barks all day long.

5 If you remember to buy it, we can post the card in the morning.

Join these pairs of sentences using *subordinating conjunctions*.

**1** The microscope isn't working.    I checked it this morning.
**2** We are going on holiday.    We have bought new suitcases.
**3** The flowers died.    I watered them every day.
**4** We saw the wrecked ship.    It had crashed on the rocks.
**5** That's the man with the dog.    He lives in the old cottage.

## Extension

Complete these sentences by adding *subordinate clauses*.

**1** He was very frightened _____.

**2** I can't go to school _____.

**3** The children had to play inside _____.

**4** I enjoyed the mystery story _____.

**5** We were almost asleep _____.

**6** She put the scissors on the table _____.

**7** He did his exercises _____.

**8** The magician pulled a rabbit out of a hat _____.

**9** The sheep were grazing in the field _____.

**10** We grow rhubarb in the garden _____.

# UNIT 11 Improving writing

We need to look very carefully at what we write to see if we can improve it.

• We can improve our writing by changing some of the vocabulary, e.g.

nice: wonderful    fantastic    amazing    exciting

said: shouted    yelled    cried    sobbed

• We can improve our writing by adding detail to our sentences, e.g.

The boy climbed the tree.    The daring boy climbed the enormous tree.

I rode my bike.    Yesterday, I reluctantly rode my bike to school.

Ask:    Use:

What kind?
How many?    — adjectives / adjective phrases / relative clauses
How much?

When?
How?    — adverbs / adverb phrases / adverb clauses
Where?
How often?

• We can improve our writing by avoiding repetition.

When we are writing about ourselves, it is very boring to begin every sentence with I, e.g.

I got up late. I was in a rush.    Getting up late, I was in a rush.
I got up late and was in a rush.

We can avoid using words that are not necessary. e.g.
Tom opened the box and put the crayons inside the box.
Tom opened the box and put the crayons inside.

 This is called ellipsis.

## Focus

Rewrite these sentences to *improve* them.
Replace the coloured words with more *interesting* ones.

**1** I walked slowly to the shops.    **2** I walked quickly to the shops.
**3** I spoke quietly.    **4** I spoke loudly.
**5** The meal was nice.    **6** The film was nice.
**7** That's a small mouse.    **8** That's a big mountain.
**9** I have got a letter.    **10** I have got a new pen.

**A** Rewrite these sentences to give *details* that answer the questions in brackets.

1 The land rover stopped on the road.     [What kind?   Where?]

2 We swam in the river.     [How?   What kind?]

3 The jug smashed.     [What kind?   When?   How?]

4 Can you see the lion?     [What kind?   Where?]

5 I ran into the shop.     [How?   What kind?   Where?]

**B** Rewrite each sentence in a shorter way to avoid repetition.

1 He drove to the shops and then he drove to the park.

2 I sat on the wall and I waited for the bus.

3 The tree was battered by the wind and eventually the tree fell over.

4 Dad is mending the car. Will you help him mend the car?

**Extension**

Look carefully at each of the sentences below.
Rewrite them so that:

- they include more *interesting vocabulary*, replacing the words *got*, *said*, *nice*, *lot*, and *big*
- they include *words*, *phrases* and *clauses* that give the reader more *detail*
- they do not begin with *I*.

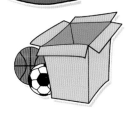

1 "Look at that!" said Lucy.

2 I got up early so I wouldn't be late.

3 This cake is nice.

4 "Where are you?" said Andrew.

5 She's a bit sad.

6 The squirrel got the nuts.

7 We got a lot of presents.

8 Where's the big box?

# UNIT 12 Nouns

A **noun** is a person, place or thing.
A **phrase** is a group of words that do not make sense on their own.
A **noun phrase** includes a **noun** and **other words** linked to it.

A **noun phrase** can begin with:

| | |
|---|---|
| definite article: | **the** cat |
| indefinite article: | **a** cat |
| demonstrative adjectives: | **that** cat / **this** cat / **those** cats / **these** cats |
| possessive adjective: | **her** cat / **their** cat |

> Words that begin noun phrases are called **determiners**.

When we mean something **specific** we can use these determiners:
definite article    demonstrative adjectives    possessive adjectives

When we mean something **general** we use the indefinite article.

A **noun phrase** can be expanded with:

| | |
|---|---|
| adjectives: | a **timid** cat / that **purring** cat |
| possessive nouns: | the **neighbour's** cat / Aunt **Sue's** cat |

## Focus

**A**  What are the *noun phrases* in each sentence?

1  The police officer's dog caught the thief.
2  Their house is on fire!
3  The long river wound its way across the plain.
4  This sandwich is made with juicy tomatoes.
5  The howling wind damaged the old chimney pot.

**B**  Make each noun into a *noun phrase* by adding the part of speech indicated.

1  _____ elephant    [definite article]
2  _____ orange      [indefinite article]
3  _____ house       [possessive noun]
4  _____ sister      [possessive adjective]
5  _____ tree        [adjective]
6  _____ tiger       [*ing* adjective]

Find the two *noun phrases* [article + noun] in each sentence.
Rewrite each sentence, expanding the noun phrases.
Underline the noun phrases.

> The first one is done for you.

1 A tree has fallen on the garage.
   <u>Their tallest tree</u> has fallen on <u>the new garage</u>.

2 The lighthouse is on the coast.
3 A lion was prowling in the grass.
4 A crowd gathered at the stadium.
5 The flag fluttered in the breeze.
6 The crows are on the lawn.
7 A car broke down in the lane.
8 The girl passed the test.

## Extension

> Noun phrases can also be made with infinitives.
> This is the runner to watch.
> That is the place to go.

> Infinitives are verb family names.

(A) What is the *noun phrase* in each sentence?

   1 That is the correct attitude to adopt.
   2 I haven't got a warm coat to wear.
   3 I need somewhere to sleep.
   4 Have you got a book to read?
   5 That's the film to watch.

(B) Write sentences with *noun phrases*.

   1 noun + to go    2 noun + to travel    3 noun + to solve

**Improving writing**

The main heading of a piece of writing has capital letters.
We usually put the main heading in the middle of the top line.
If we use subheadings to divide our writing, we use a capital letter for each important word.

---
### All About the Wind

In the 19th century, Sir Francis Beaufort worked out what happens when the wind moves at different speeds.
**Types of Wind**
Wind can be a force 0, right up to a force 12.
---

As well as subheadings, we can use other devices to help organise our writing.
• Bullet points. Use capital letters and full stops for full sentences.

---
- **Types of Wind**
  Wind can be a force 0, right up to a force 12.
- **Effect of the Wind**
  Different things happen depending on the wind speed.
- **Speed**
  Winds can blow at less than 1 kph to over 117 kph.
---

- Charts

This is the Beaufort Scale.

| Force | Type of wind | What you can see | Speed |
|---|---|---|---|
| 0 | calm | smoke rises straight up | 0 kph |
| 1 | light air | smoke drifts | 1–5 kph |
| 2 | light breeze | leaves rustle/weather vane moves | 6–11 kph |

**Focus**

Answer the questions.
1 What should always come at the top of a piece of writing?
2 In what three ways can you organise information in your writing?
3 How do you think using devices to organise writing helps the reader?
4 Why do you think it is called the Beaufort Scale?
5 Find an example of a chart in a non-fiction book and discuss what it tells you.

## Practice

Here is the rest of the information you need to complete the Beaufort Scale.

| |
|---|
| force 7 / near gale / whole trees bend over / 50–61 kph |

| |
|---|
| force 3 / gentle breeze / twigs move and flags flap / 12–19 kph |

| |
|---|
| force II / violent storm / general destruction / 103–117 kph |

| |
|---|
| force 8 / gale / twigs break off / 62–74 kph |

| |
|---|
| force 5 / fresh breeze / small trees start to sway / 30–39 kph |

| |
|---|
| force 10 / storm / trees uprooted, buildings badly damaged / 89–102 kph |

| |
|---|
| force 4 / moderate breeze / dust and paper blown about, small branches move / 20–29 kph |

| |
|---|
| force 6 / strong breeze / large branches move / 40–49 kph |

| |
|---|
| force 9 / strong gale / chimneys and slates fall / 75–88 kph |

| |
|---|
| force 12 / hurricane/coastal flooding and devastation / II8 kph |

Use the information for force 0, 1 and 2 on the previous page.

Sort out the correct order for the information above.

Draw and complete a chart for the Beaufort Scale.

## Extension

Choose three animals to research. Find out about:
- where they live – habitat
- what they look like – description
- what they eat – diet.

Make notes on the information you find.

Show the information in a chart. Your chart should have:
- a main heading
- columns and column headings.

Some words are very confusing!

- **who's and whose**

  who     = who is / who has
  **Who's** that at the door?

  whose   = relative pronoun – belonging to
  There was a boy **whose** name was Jim.

- **you're and your**

  you're  = you are
  **You're** soaking wet!

  your    = possessive adjective
  Is this **your** umbrella?

- **fewer and less**

  fewer   = adjective with nouns that can be counted
  There are **fewer** people here than last time.

  less    = adjective with nouns that cannot be counted
  Could I have **less** milk in my tea?

- **weather and whether**

  weather = noun
  The **weather** is very good today.

  whether = conjunction
  I do not know **whether** it's going to rain or not.

### Focus

Discuss and correct the *mistake* in each sentence.

1 Whose coming to play football?
2 You're story was very exciting.
3 There are less cars in the village now they have built the bypass.
4 I'm not sure weather I want to go or not.
5 There's fewer time than I thought.
6 I think your going to be late!
7 We had very good whether on our holidays.
8 I don't know who's this book is.

## Practice

**A** Copy and complete the sentences with *who's* or *whose*.

1 The man _____ car was damaged is furious.

2 _____ taken the last biscuit?

3 I know _____ responsible for the mess.

**B** Copy and complete the sentences with *your* or *you're*.

1 If _____ very tired, go to bed.

2 What's _____ name?

3 If _____ certain, I'll take _____ word for it.

**C** Copy and complete the sentences with *fewer* or *less*.

1 That checkout says 'Five items or _____'.

2 If you eat _____ sugar, you will be healthier.

3 If you spend _____ time, you will sell _____ tickets.

**D** Copy and complete the sentences with *weather* or *whether*.

1 The _____ is unusual for this time of year.

2 I'm wondering _____ to play tennis or not.

3 I don't know _____ the _____ will be good or not.

## Extension

Write a sentence that contains each pair of words.

| | | | | |
|---|---|---|---|---|
| **1** its | it's | | **2** win | beat |
| **3** of | have | | **4** teach | learn |
| **5** lend | borrow | | **6** there | their |

# Punctuation

A **hyphen** is a small dash used between words.
amiable-looking

- **compound nouns**

  These can be:  one word  – sunbed

  two words  – sun cream

  hyphenated  – sun-bonnet

- **compound verbs**

  These can be:  one word  – to waterproof

  hyphenated  – to water-ski

- **compound adjectives**

  These are:  hyphenated  – sweet-tasting

  two-seater

- **adverbs NOT ending in** *ly*

  These form compound words in front of a noun: well-known

  good-looking

- **numbers**

  All numbers from 21 to 99:  twenty-one

  ninety-nine

- **fractions**

  All fractions, e.g. $\frac{1}{4}$, $\frac{2}{3}$, are hyphenated: one-quarter

  two-thirds

Better check in a dictionary!

Use a comma, not a hyphen, between two adjectives if you can put *and* between them.

**Focus**

In each group of *compound nouns*, one is one word, one is two words, and one is hyphenated. Which is which?

**1** **a** film clip  **b** film maker  **c** film set

**2** **a** sea anchor  **b** sea angel  **c** sea bed

**3** **a** land yacht  **b** land slide  **c** land wind

**4** **a** rain drop  **b** rain cloud  **c** rain worm

Use a dictionary to help.

Copy these *compound words*.
Some need *hyphenating*. Some are one word.

Use a dictionary to help.

1  **a** light fingered       **b** light hearted       **c** light house
2  **a** wet suit             **b** wet land            **c** wet weather
3  **a** team mate            **b** team teaching        **c** team work
4  **a** drift net            **b** drift ice           **c** drift wood
5  **a** cheese burger        **b** cheese cutter        **c** cheese cake

**Extension**

Look at these newspaper headlines.
Each one should include a *hyphen*.
Explain what each one means without the hyphen.

**HEAVY METAL DETECTOR
FINDS TREASURE TROVE**

**Small business men
launch new superstore**

**Foreign car dealer
goes under**

**Man eating
snakes spotted
in village**

Copy each headline and include the hyphen.
Explain what each one means with the hyphen.

Direct speech is when we write the actual words that someone says.

- speech marks go at the beginning and the end of the spoken words
- punctuation at the end of the spoken words goes before the speech marks
- when a different person speaks, we begin a new line.

> "Do you know where the Houses of Parliament are?" asked Oscar.
>
> Peter thought for a while. "In London, I think."

Sometimes we split the spoken words, so we have to be very careful with the punctuation.

**1** "I would like to visit Egypt," said Ken, "because the photos of the ancient pyramids are amazing!"

The sentence has been split by the words *said Ken*, so we use two sets of speech marks and put a comma after *said Ken*.

**2** "I would like to visit Egypt," said Ken. "The photos I've seen of the ancient pyramids are amazing!"

This time, Ken says two sentences. We still use two sets of speech marks but we put a full stop after *said Ken* before we begin a new sentence.

**Focus**

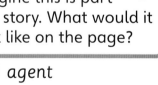

Imagine this is part of a story. What would it look like on the page?

Copy and punctuate the *direct speech sentences*. Set this out as a conversation.

1 Have you visited Australia before asked the travel agent
2 Harry replied I was there when I was three
3 So said the travel agent I don't suppose you remember much about it
4 Not much agreed Harry I do remember it was very hot
5 Where did you stay the travel agent inquired
6 We stayed in Sydney said Harry and I think we went on to Melbourne
7 Where to this time asked the travel agent
8 Ayers Rock and Alice Springs said Harry I'm really looking forward to travelling across the desert

Copy and finish each sentence with what you think the speaker *might say*.
Add the missing *punctuation*.

1 They've landed in Smuggler's Cove shouted the fisherman
   and _____

2 That rabbit's cage needs a thorough clean said Dad so _____

3 The television programme was interrupted said Mum
   because _____

4 _____ said the gardener until I've dug up the weeds

5 _____ asked Fred although I think you are wrong.

## Extension

Indirect speech is when we write about what someone has said.

Indirect speech is also called reported speech.

- We don't use the actual spoken words.
- We don't use speech marks.

**direct speech**

"I like this cake," said Maria.

"The chimney is falling," shouted the fireman.

**indirect speech**

Maria said that she liked the cake.

The fireman shouted that the chimney was falling.

A Write a conversation in *direct speech* between a travel agent and a customer who is booking a holiday.

Choose a place you would like to visit.

Remember to:

- use *speech marks* and other *punctuation*
- begin a *new line* when a different person speaks
- use synonyms for *said*.

B Write the same conversation in *indirect speech*.

Remember that you do NOT need speech marks because you are not writing the actual words that were spoken.

**Verbs**

Sometimes verbs are made up of more than one word.
Some verbs are made up of a modal verb + a main verb.
This group of modal verbs is very useful.

| | | |
|---|---|---|
| may | might | could |
| can | must | would |
| | | should |

Modal verbs are
helper verbs.

My brother can ride a bicycle.
You may ride my bicycle.
You must learn to ride a bicycle.
I might ride my bicycle to school.
I could ride my bicycle if I mended the tyre.
I would ride my bicycle if it wasn't raining.
I should ride my bicycle more often.

Here are some more useful auxiliary verbs.

have/has to     ought to     have/has got to     had better

I have to learn these spellings.
I ought to learn these spellings.
I have got to learn these spellings.
I had better learn these spellings.

**Focus**

What is the *auxiliary verb* in each sentence?

1   I had better water the plants before they all die!

2   You ought to take more care of yourself.

3   I have got to warn him before it is too late.

4   He had better do as he is told this time!

5   It has got to stop raining soon!

6   She has to go to the dentist.

7   They ought to keep to the footpath.

8   We have to win this match.

**A** Copy and complete the sentences with *must* or *ought to*.

**1** They _____ look at the map but I don't think they will!

**2** I'm so hungry I _____ have something to eat.

**3** You can play in the garden but you _____ not go into the lane.

**4** Do you think we _____ phone an ambulance?

**B** Copy and complete the sentences with *have to*, *has to* or *had better*.

**1** He _____ meet his friends at one o'clock.

**2** The neighbours _____ turn the music down or I will phone the police!

**3** She _____ hurry or the coach will go without her.

**4** Nurses _____ work at the weekend.

**Extension**

Write a sentence about what you:

**1** should do
**2** can do
**3** may do
**4** ought to do
**5** have to do
**6** have got to do

When the subject of a sentence does the action of the verb, the verb is called an active verb.

The man bought a ticket.

| subject | verb | object |

In this sentence, bought is an active verb.

When the subject of the sentence has the action done to it, the verb is called a passive verb.

The ticket was bought by the man.

| subject | verb | object |

In a passive sentence, the agent is the person or thing doing the action.

In this sentence, was bought is a passive verb.

**Focus**

Find the *verb* in each sentence.
Say whether it is an *active verb* or a *passive verb*.

1   The judge banged the table.

2   A sailor was hit by the rigging.

3   A few regular customers went into the shop every day.

4   The monster attacked the town.

5   One of the escalators was stopped by the shop manager.

6   The bridge fell into the river.

7   The library was broken into by a thief.

8   I have lost my dictionary.

## Practice

**A** Rewrite each of the sentences, changing them from *active* to *passive*.

The first one is done for you.

**1** Our teacher read the class a story.

A story was read to the class by a teacher.

**2** The captain won a famous victory.

**3** The hikers heard thunder in the afternoon.

**4** Lucy tidied the room yesterday.

**5** The striker scored a goal.

**B** Rewrite each of the sentences, changing them from *passive* to *active*.

The first one is done for you.

**1** The new vase was cracked by the boy.

The boy cracked the new vase.

**2** The windows were cleaned this morning by my dad.

**3** The play was disliked by the audience.

**4** The house was shaded by the trees.

**5** Rabbits are shot by some farmers.

## Extension

**A** Write sentences where each of the verbs is *active*.

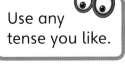
Use any tense you like.

**1** to carry    **2** to lift    **3** to see

**4** to write    **5** to cover    **6** to bury

**B** Rewrite your sentences from **A**, making the verbs *passive*.

# Standard and Non-standard English

When we write for an audience, we use Standard English.

This is so that, whatever part of the country our readers are from, they can understand what we have written.

When we write for ourselves or have a conversation with people we know, we often use Non-standard English.

Non-standard English is also known as slang.

| Standard English | Non-standard English |
| --- | --- |
| It's very cold. | It's right cold. |
| I haven't got a scarf. | I ain't got a scarf. |
| I haven't got any gloves. | I ain't got no gloves. |
| I'm freezing. | I'm freezin. |
| I need a scarf and some gloves. | I need a scarf an some gloves. |

## Focus

Each of these sentences is written in Non-standard English. How would they be written in *Standard English*?

1. We're gonna be late for school.
2. That goal was ace!
3. The park keeper told us to buzz off.
4. You do talk a load of rubbish!
5. I think these shoes are cool.
6. He's stuffed!
7. You're always picking on me.
8. The thief stashed the loot in his garage.
9. That's wicked!
10. I'm really fed up.

**A** Each sentence contains a *noun* that is Non-standard English.
Copy the sentences, changing the nouns into *Standard English*.

1 May I have some more spuds?
2 That cost me five quid!
3 Who was that bloke you were talking to?
4 Our neighbours have seven kids.
5 The old dears like the park.
6 This is my favourite grub!
7 He wants to be a copper when he grows up.
8 The guys in the football team are really good.

**B** Each sentence contains a word that is *Non-standard English*.
Copy the sentences, changing the word into *Standard English*.

1 I'm sure that ain't right.
2 We had a right good time.
3 He's tired coz he didn't sleep very well.
4 They gotter win the match.
5 She's gonna have a party at the weekend.
6 Are you tellin me the truth?

**Extension**

Cockney rhyming slang is interesting. A Cockney is someone who is born within the sound of the bells of St Mary Le Bow church in East London.

apples and pears = stairs
tea leaf = thief

These are Cockney rhyming slang for parts of the body.
Can you work them out?

1 mince pies          2 clothes pegs          3 loaf of bread

4 north and south     5 brass bands           6 plates of meat

7 biscuits and cheese 8 Chevy Chase           9 Hampstead Heath

# Sentences

We can use conditional clauses in sentences when one thing depends on another.

> The swallows will nest here if we leave them alone.

> The swallows nesting here depends on us leaving them alone.

> Pandas will die out unless we save them.

> Pandas not dying out depends on us saving them.

A conditional clause begins with a conjunction.

Here are some useful conjunctions.

| if | unless | provided |
|---|---|---|
| if only | on condition that | providing that |
| only if | as long as | assuming that |

The conjunction can be one word or a phrase.

## Focus

What is the *conditional clause* in each sentence?

1 The old man will go fishing as long as the weather remains fine.

2 I'm going into town assuming I can get a bus.

3 The house will not be finished this month unless the builders work more quickly.

4 I will call in the morning only if I have news.

5 The concert will go ahead provided that no more of the cast becomes ill.

6 You can watch the film on condition that you go to bed as soon as it has finished.

7 Sports day will be great fun if it doesn't rain!

8 She doesn't like carrots unless they are roasted.

Use as many different conjunctions as you can.

Copy and complete the sentences with suitable *conditional clauses*.

1  The village will be destroyed by fire _____.
2  We can't climb the mountain, _____.
3  You can have your friends for tea _____.
4  The famous pianist agreed to play _____.
5  The workers were to get a raise _____.

**Extension**

> Like adverb clauses, conditional clauses can come at the beginning of a sentence.
>
>    The fox will get into the chicken house unless we repair it.
>
>    Unless we repair the chicken house, the fox will get in.

Complete each sentence with a *conditional clause*.

Use each *conjunction* in the box only once.

> only if     assuming that     unless     as long as     if

1  _____, the ships will crash onto the rocks.
2  _____, we cannot go on holiday!
3  _____, can we go to the concert?
4  _____, you can borrow my bicycle.
5  _____, we will leave this afternoon.

# Punctuation

The **semicolon ;** and the **colon :** are mainly used in formal writing.

- A **semicolon** separates **two or more statements** which are related to each other in a sentence. The sentence would still make sense if we used a **conjunction**.

  > The house was very spooky; the wind whistled through the broken windows.

  > The house was very spooky **and** the wind whistled through the broken windows.

A **semicolon** can also be used instead of a comma for **items in a list** where the items are **more than one word**.

  > There were many animals in the zoo: stately giraffes with their long, graceful necks; lumbering elephants plodding around the enclosure; mischievous monkeys chattering and swinging from the branches; brightly coloured parrots squawking and talking.

- The **colon** is used to introduce a list.

  > You will need the following: eggs, flour, milk, sugar and butter.

  A **colon** is also used to **introduce a result**, or instead of **for example**.

  > The committee made a decision: it would fund the new sports centre.

  > We have some things to discuss: the cost and the time it will take.

  A **colon** is also used to **balance one statement against another**.

  > Jim remembered his passport: Tom forgot his.

## Focus

**A** Say why a *semicolon* has been used in these sentences.

1 The shops were busy; people were in search of a bargain.
2 Sam thought about all he had to do: feed the rabbits; take the dog for a walk; get the car serviced; mow the lawn.

**B** Say why a *colon* has been used in these sentences.

1 Remember to bring: pens, pencils, a ruler, a rubber and a notebook.
2 The choice was made: the Christmas pantomime would be *Cinderella*.
3 Arguing doesn't solve anything: talking sensibly does.

Copy and *punctuate* these sentences.

1 Young men play football older men play golf.
2 The park looked beautiful gardeners worked tirelessly through the seasons.

Semicolons and colons are missing.

3 We need a good striker someone from the Premier League.
4 Kim looked around down the High Street many well-known shops had closed litter blew about the once tidy streets graffiti scarred the walls.
5 The fire alarm went off the fire brigade was quickly on the scene.

## Extension

In less formal writing, you can use a dash to introduce further information instead of a colon.

All the apples were the same – red and juicy.

Using *semicolons*, *colons* and *dashes*, write sentences about:

1 a high wind and a fallen tree
2 a detailed list of what you did in school yesterday
3 a list of fruit to buy in the supermarket
4 Mum and Dad making a decision about something, and what that decision is
5 the sort of place you would like to go on holiday, and an example
6 one person doing something – another person doing the opposite.

# Paragraphs

Discursive writing is when you look at both sides of an argument.

A **paragraph** is a **group of sentences** about one main idea.

Having **paragraphs** in **discursive writing** makes it easier for the reader to follow.

There are usually many points **for** and **against** any subject.

We write about each point in **a new paragraph**.

We **link** the paragraphs with phrases such as:

In my view ...    On the other hand ...    In addition ...

We have an **introductory paragraph** so the reader knows what the subject is.

We have a **concluding paragraph** to sum up for the reader.

## Should Animals Be Kept in Zoos?

**introductory paragraph** → Some people are in favour of zoos. Others think that it is cruel and unnatural.

**paragraph 2** → One argument for having zoos is that we can see animals from all over the world. Most people would never get to see these animals in the wild.

**paragraph 3** → In addition, zoos protect animals. Many species would have become extinct if they had not been able to breed in zoos.

**paragraph 4** → On the other hand, animals in zoos are not free. They cannot roam about as they would in the wild.

**paragraph 5** → Consequently, they do not behave naturally as they do not have to hunt for their food or protect themselves from predators.

**concluding paragraph** → To sum up, some people think animals are better off in their natural habitat and should take their chances in the wild. Others, however, think zoos do useful work and protect endangered species.

## Focus

Look at each *paragraph* in turn.

**1** How is it started?

**2** What point is it making?

**3** How many arguments for zoos does the writer include?

**4** How many arguments against zoos does the writer include?

## Practice

Write a short *discursive* piece with the title:
*Are Mobile Phones a Good or Bad Thing?*

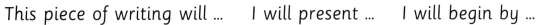

* Think about the introductory paragraph.

Here are some useful ways to begin.

> This piece of writing will …     I will present …     I will begin by …

* Think of *two reasons* why mobile phones are *a good thing*.

Here are some useful ways to begin.

> One opinion is that …     In addition …     Let's consider …

* Think of *two reasons* why mobile phones are *a bad thing*.

Here are some useful ways to begin.

> Another point of view is …     Many people disagree …

* Think about the *concluding paragraph*.

Here are some useful ways to begin.

> To sum up …     It is clear that …

## Extension

Choose one of the following and write a *discursive* piece with six paragraphs.

> Video games – good or bad?

> Sports day – good or bad?

> School uniform – good or bad?

* introductory paragraph:     what you are writing about.
* second paragraph:     first reason **for**
* third paragraph:     second reason **for**
* fourth paragraph:     first reason **against**
* fifth paragraph:     second reason **against**
* concluding paragraph:     sum up

Use this paragraph plan.

# Verbs

When the **subject** of a sentence does **the action of the verb**, the verb is called an **active** verb.

The eagle built a nest.

In this sentence, **built** is an **active** verb.

When the **subject** of the sentence has **the action done to it**, the verb is called a passive verb.

The nest was built by the eagle.

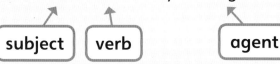

In a passive sentence, the **agent** is the person or thing **doing the action**.

In this sentence, **was built** is a **passive** verb.

Sometimes in a **passive sentence**, the **agent** is not included.

The window was broken.

We don't know who or what broke the window.

It's a mystery!

## Focus

Say which of these sentences has an *active* verb and which has a *passive* verb.

1 The soldier was hidden by the bushes.
2 The yacht sailed into the harbour.
3 The booking was taken by the restaurant manager.
4 Competitors were given a number by the organiser.
5 My neighbour keeps bees.
6 The birds are frequently chased by the cat.

## Practice

**A** All of these sentences have passive verbs but no agents.
Copy each sentence and add a *suitable agent*.

**1** The painting was completed.
**2** The cows are milked every morning.
**3** The traffic was held up.
**4** The curtains were drawn.
**5** Everyone was congratulated.

**B** Copy and complete these *passive sentences*.

**1** _____ by the mysterious stranger.
**2** _____ by our uncle.
**3** _____ by two fierce swans.
**4** _____ by a meteor.
**5** _____ by a hawk.

## Extension

These are pairs of *subjects* and *objects*.
Write an *active sentence* using each pair.
Write a *passive sentence* using each pair.

| | subject | object |
|---|---|---|
| **1** | baker | cake |
| **2** | postman | parcel |
| **3** | shopper | bargain |
| **4** | secretary | minutes |
| **5** | lightning | tree |

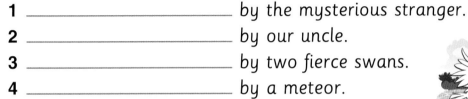

# Standard English

When we **write for an audience**, we use **Standard English**.

This is so that, whatever part of the country our readers are from, they can understand what we have written.

When we **write for ourselves** or have a **conversation** with people we know, we often use **Non-standard English**.

In writing, we must be careful with:

- double negatives

  I didn't do nothing. ✗       I didn't do anything. ✓

- mixing up words

  May I lend that book. ✗       May I borrow that book? ✓

  Will you learn me? ✗       Will you teach me? ✓

  I could of come. ✗       I could have come. ✓

  Me and my friends play netball. ✗       My friends and I play netball. ✓

  This is the letter what I wrote. ✗       This is the letter that I wrote. ✓

- noun/verb agreement

  We was tired. ✗       We were tired. ✓

  I is curious. ✗       I am curious. ✓

  They is the winners. ✗       They are the winners. ✓

You must also be careful with:

- them/those

  Them are my shoes. ✗       Those are my shoes. ✓

- me/my

  I can't find me keys. ✗       I can't find my keys. ✓

## Focus

Each sentence below is written in Non-standard English.
How would they be written in *Standard English*?

1  I don't want nothing to eat.

2  Would you borrow me a pencil?

3  He learned me to speak French.

4  We should of left earlier.

5  Me and my brother like cricket.

6  Give me the key what you found.

7  The tigers was hungry.

8  You was so noisy!

9  We is the best team.

10  Them are beautiful flowers.

11  They has gone on holiday.

12  I need me glasses.

## Practice

**A** Copy and complete the sentences with the correct word from the brackets.

**1** I _____ books from the library.    (lend/borrow)

**2** Will you put _____ flowers in a vase.    (them/those)

**3** We should _____ brought an umbrella.    (have/of)

**4** Can you tell me _____ time it is?    (that/what)

**5** I would like a packet _____ biscuits.    (have/of)

**6** Give me the plate _____ you broke.    (that/what)

**7** Will you _____ me that DVD?    (lend/borrow)

**8** I saw _____ outside the shop.    (them/those)

**B** Rewrite the sentences in *Standard English*.

**1** Me and Mum go shopping on Saturday.

**2** Sam never goes nowhere.

**3** The elephants is huge!

**4** I would of been on time but the bus broke down.

**5** She go to her friend's house after school.

## Extension

Tom and Ben are talking on their mobile phones.

They are using *Non-standard English*.

Continue their conversation in Non-standard English.

Give each boy at least four more things to say.

Rewrite their conversation in *Standard English*.

Remember to set out the conversation correctly, and use speech marks and any other necessary punctuation.

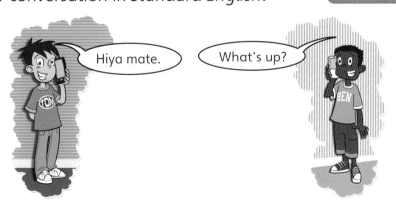

Hiya mate.

What's up?

# Punctuation

A **hyphen** is a small dash used between words. e.g.

- compound nouns          sun-bonnet
- compound verbs          to water-ski
- compound adjectives     hair-raising
- adverbs NOT ending in *ly*   well-known
- numbers                 twenty-one
- fractions               one-quarter

A **hyphen** can also be used with **prefixes**.

Always check with a dictionary!

- prefix + hyphen + proper noun, e.g. **un-American**
- If the prefix ends in a **vowel** and the word begins with the **same vowel**, use a hyphen.

  sem**i**-**i**nvalid
  pr**e**-**e**lection
  c**o**-**o**pt

Most **semi** words are hyphenated.

- Use a hyphen with all words beginning with **self**, except **selfish**, **selfsame** and **selfless**.

  **self**-respect
  **self**-addressed

- Use a hyphen with the prefix **ex** when it means **no longer**.

  **ex**-wife
  **ex**-colleague

- Use a hyphen with the prefix **re** when it means **again**.

  **re**-cover
  **re**-count

## Focus

Where should the *hyphen* go?

| | | |
|---|---|---|
| **1** expresident | **2** coown | **3** exservice |
| **4** preestablish | **5** selfadhesive | **6** semidetached |
| **7** antiinflammatory | **8** reroof | **9** excon |
| **10** semifinal | **11** antiBritish | **12** selfaware |

**A** Write a *hyphenated word* that begins with each of these *prefixes*.

1 un          2 pre

3 ex          4 co

5 semi        6 self

Use a dictionary to help you find hyphenated words.

**B** Put each of your hyphenated words in sentences of your own.

## Extension

We use a hyphen with the prefix re meaning again.

There are some re words that mean one thing with a hyphen and something very different with no hyphen.

The chair is very shabby so I must re-cover it.

I hope you recover from your illness soon.

**A** Write a sentence using each of these words *without a hyphen*.

1 reserve       2 recollect

3 recount       4 resent

5 resign        6 redress

7 repress       8 rebound

**B** Add a *hyphen* to each word.

**C** Write a sentence using each of these words *with a hyphen*.

Sentences contain clauses.

- A main clause is a sentence in itself.    The gardener pruned the roses.

  | | |
  |---|---|
  | It has a subject | = The gardener |
  | It has a predicate | = pruned the roses |
  | It has a proper verb in the predicate | = pruned |

- An adverb clause tells us more about the verb in the main clause.
  An adverb clause begins with a conjunction.
  The gardener pruned the roses so that they would bloom again.

  | | | |
  |---|---|---|
  | main clause | = | The gardener pruned the roses |
  | adverb clause | = | so that they would bloom again |

- A relative clause tells us more about the noun in the main clause.
  A relative clause begins with a relative pronoun.
  The gardener pruned the roses that grew around the door.

  | | | |
  |---|---|---|
  | main clause | = | The gardener pruned the roses |
  | relative clause | = | that grew around the door |

- A conditional clause is when one thing depends on another.
  The gardener will prune the roses if they get too straggly.
  Conditional clauses begin with conjunctions such as:

  | | | |
  |---|---|---|
  | if | unless | provided |
  | if only | on condition that | providing that |
  | only if | as long as | assuming that |

## Focus

A relative clause is also known as an adjective clause.

Copy the sentences. Underline the *main clauses*.

1 That boat won the race although the sail was damaged.

2 She read the book that had been recommended.

3 We can fly the kite unless the wind drops.

4 The twins could go on the trip provided they saved their pocket money.

5 The gardener who pruned the roses works hard.

Copy and complete the sentences as indicated.

**1** (adverb clause)＿＿＿＿＿, I don't know *the registration number.*

**2** I will never get this finished ＿＿＿＿＿ (conditional clause).

**3** The pirate buried the treasure ＿＿＿＿＿ (relative clause).

**4** (conditional clause) ＿＿＿＿＿ you can leave early.

**5** I must learn to swim ＿＿＿＿＿ (adverb clause).

**6** Our new Head Teacher is a woman ＿＿＿＿＿ (relative clause).

## Extension

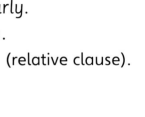

**A** Copy and complete each sentence in two ways:

The first one is done for you.

- by adding an *adverb clause*
- by adding a *relative clause*.

**1** *The dog chased the rabbit.*

adverb clause: The dog chased the rabbit *after it popped up from its burrow.*

relative clause: The dog chased the rabbit *that lived in the garden.*

**2** People went to the concert.

**3** Adventurers climb mountains.

**4** We met his brother.

**5** An iceberg sunk the Titanic.

**B** Use the sentence beginnings from **A**.

Complete each one with a *conditional clause*, making any changes necessary.

**1** The dog *will chase* the rabbit *if it comes too near.*

# Verbs

The passive form of a verb is usually used in formal speech and writing.

    active:      The committee outvoted the chairman.
    passive:    The chairman was outvoted by the committee.

Another verb form that is only used in formal speech and writing, is the subjunctive.

    The manager recommended that he join the company.
    It was important that the voters be at the meeting.

The subjunctive form of the verb is the same as the verb family name without the 'to'.

The verb family name is the infinitive.

| **verb family name** | to start | to vote | to be |
|---|---|---|---|
| **subjunctive** | start | vote | be |

That + subjunctive is often used with these:

- verbs        ask       command     demand    insist
                 propose    recommend    request     suggest

- expressions    it is desirable     it is essential      it is important
                 it is necessary    it is a good idea    it is a bad idea

The subjunctive form is always the same. It does not matter whether the sentence is present or past.

| He asks that the people stay quiet. | present |
| He asked that the people stay quiet. | past |
| It is important that everyone be polite. | present |
| It was important that everyone be polite. | past |

## Focus

Read each pair of sentences. Which one uses the *subjunctive*?

1 You must go home.                      I insist that you go home.

2 It was great that you finished the test.    It was important that you finish the test.

3 It is a good idea that she send the letter.   Great idea that she sends the letter!

4 Jill wanted us to go to her party.       Jill requested that we attend her party.

5 I suggest that you stop eating chocolate.   You should stop eating chocolate.

6 Don't swim in the sea today.            It is recommended that you don't swim in the sea today.

## Practice

**A** Rewrite these active sentences as *passive sentences*.

1 Everyone on board wore life jackets.
2 The speaker delivered an interesting talk.
3 The rough sea swamped the boat.
4 Fire damaged several buildings.
5 Voters elected a new Mayor.

**B** Rewrite these sentences using the *subjunctive form*.

1 He is recommending great changes.
2 She suggested that she needed an assistant.
3 The doctor suggested that they swam everyday.
4 I insisted he should leave immediately.
5 They proposed longer working days.

## Extension

For very formal speech and writing, we use the subjunctive form of were instead of was with I, he, she and it.

informal:   If I was you, I'd take the chance.

formal:      If I were you, I would take the chance.

Notice as well that in formal speech and writing, we don't use contractions.

Write these informal sentences *formally*.

1 If I was the Head Teacher, I'd let Sports Day go ahead.
2 I wish I was more successful.
3 If he was you, he'd do the same.
4 If it was only that simple, everyone could do it.
5 She wished it was the weekend.

When we write Standard English we should not use slang, and we should be very careful with our grammar.

**Non-standard English**

We was right pleased.

I like them shoes coz there red.

**Standard English**

We were very pleased.

I like those shoes because they are red.

It is very important to use Standard English when we are speaking or writing in formal situations.

- Here is a text message from one friend to another. This is informal.

    how r u? im gr8

- Here is an email from a girl to her sister. This is informal.

    Hi Sis How are things? Pretty dull here. Going shopping with Mum later – hope she'll buy me some stuff! Skype later? Beth

- Here is a letter Beth's sister has written to go with a job application. This is formal.

> 21 Brook Close
> Manchester
> 12.08.14
>
> Dear Sir,
>
> Please find enclosed my application form for the post of manager.
>
> It has always been my ambition to work for your company and I trust that my CV and previous experience will be of interest to you.
>
> Should you wish to meet with me, I would be delighted to come for an interview at your convenience.
>
> I also enclose references for your attention, given by my current employers.
>
> Yours faithfully,
> Lorraine Bow

**Focus**

Read the text message, email and the letter.

Discuss the differences between the *three types of writing*.

## Practice

**A** Think about *text messaging*.

Rewrite the text message on the previous page for an older relative who does not understand textspeak.

Write your own text message to a friend.

Rewrite it for your older relative.

**B** Think about *emailing*.

Rewrite the email on the previous page in Standard English.

Write your own email to a friend.

Rewrite it in Standard English.

> Imagine your teacher is going to mark it!

**C** Think about *letter writing*.

Read the letter on the previous page again.

What *words* and *phrases* has the writer used instead of the following?

**1** It's in the envelope

**2** the job

**3** I've always wanted to

**4** I think

**5** what I've done before

**6** If you want to meet up

**7** it would be OK

**8** when it suits

**9** there's some references

**10** the people I work for now.

## Extension

> Think carefully about the vocabulary you will use.

Choose one of these subjects to write about.

My pet          My holiday          My hobby

Write a *text message* to a close friend.

Write an *email* to an older relative.

Write a *letter* to an older relative who always speaks and writes in Standard English.

# How to use this book

The heading tells you what the grammar topic is.

The information box tells you about the grammar topic.

The owl gives you extra information.

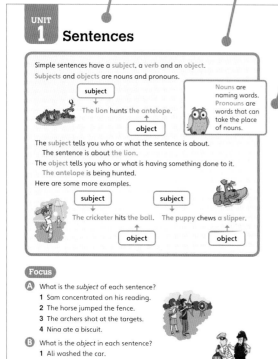

**UNIT 1**

## Sentences

Simple sentences have a subject, a verb and an object.
Subjects and objects are nouns and pronouns.

subject
↓
The lion hunts the antelope.
↑
object

Nouns are naming words. Pronouns are words that can take the place of nouns.

The subject tells you who or what the sentence is about.
The sentence is about the lion.
The object tells you who or what is having something done to it.
The antelope is being hunted.
Here are some more examples.

subject
↓
The cricketer hits the ball.
↑
object

subject
↓
The puppy chews a slipper.
↑
object

**Focus**

Ⓐ What is the *subject* of each sentence?
1 Sam concentrated on his reading.
2 The horse jumped the fence.
3 The archers shot at the targets.
4 Nina ate a biscuit.

Ⓑ What is the *object* in each sentence?
1 Ali washed the car.
2 My friends bought me a present.
3 Policemen catch robbers.
4 The spider devoured the fly.

6

**Practice**

Copy and finish each sentence by adding an interesting *object* to each one.
1 Kali grabbed _____.
2 The young girl spilt _____.
3 Frank bought some _____.
4 The giraffe ate _____.
5 My cousin made _____.

**Extension**

Ⓐ Copy the sentences into your book.
Make each one more interesting by adding an *adjective* in front of each *subject* and each *object*.
1 The man ate the pie.
2 The decorator painted the wall.
3 The boy flew his kite.
4 The cobra hissed at the woman.
5 Blackbirds eat worms.

Ⓑ Write sentences of your own using these pairs of *subjects* and *objects*.

Make your sentences interesting by using adjectives.

| subject | object |
|---------|--------|
| 1 cat | tree |
| 2 pirate | treasure |
| 3 musician | song |
| 4 bird | nest |
| 5 policewoman | traffic |

7

You might want to discuss these questions with a talk partner before answering them.

The tips box tells you more about answering the question.

Sometimes your teacher might ask you to fill in Activity Sheets.

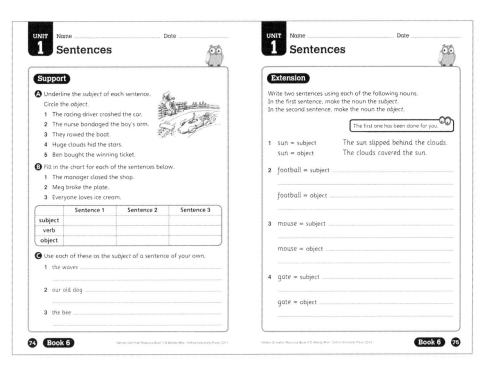

UNIT 1 Name _____ Date _____

## Sentences

**Support**

Ⓐ Underline the *subject* of each sentence. Circle the *object*.
1 The racing driver crashed the car.
2 The nurse bandaged the boy's arm.
3 They rowed the boat.
4 Huge clouds hid the stars.
5 Ben bought the winning ticket.

Ⓑ Fill in the chart for each of the sentences below.
1 The manager closed the shop.
2 Meg broke the plate.
3 Everyone loves ice cream.

|  | Sentence 1 | Sentence 2 | Sentence 3 |
|---|---|---|---|
| subject |  |  |  |
| verb |  |  |  |
| object |  |  |  |

Ⓒ Use each of these as the *subject* of a sentence of your own.
1 the waves _____
2 our old dog _____
3 the bee _____

74 **Book 6**

UNIT 1 Name _____ Date _____

## Sentences

**Extension**

Write two sentences using each of the following nouns.
In the first sentence, make the noun the *subject*.
In the second sentence, make the noun the *object*.

The first one has been done for you.

1 sun = subject    The sun slipped behind the clouds.
  sun = object     The clouds covered the sun.

2 football = subject _____

  football = object _____

3 mouse = subject _____

  mouse = object _____

4 gate = subject _____

  gate = object _____

**Book 6** 75

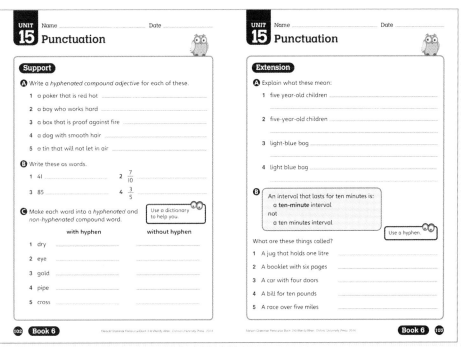

UNIT 15 Name _____ Date _____

## Punctuation

**Support**

Ⓐ Write a *hyphenated compound adjective* for each of these.
1 a poker that is red hot _____
2 a boy who works hard _____
3 a box that is proof against fire _____
4 a dog with smooth hair _____
5 a tin that will not let in air _____

Ⓑ Write these as words.
1 4l _____    2 $\frac{7}{10}$ _____
3 85 _____    4 $\frac{3}{5}$ _____

Ⓒ Make each word into a *hyphenated* and *non-hyphenated* compound word.

Use a dictionary to help you.

|  | with hyphen | without hyphen |
|---|---|---|
| 1 dry |  |  |
| 2 eye |  |  |
| 3 gold |  |  |
| 4 pipe |  |  |
| 5 cross |  |  |

102 **Book 6**

UNIT 15 Name _____ Date _____

## Punctuation

**Extension**

Ⓐ Explain what these mean:
1 five year-old children _____
2 five-year-old children _____
3 light-blue bag _____
4 light blue bag _____

Ⓑ An interval that lasts for ten minutes is:
  a **ten-minute** interval
  not
  a ten minutes interval

Use a hyphen.

What are these things called?
1 A jug that holds one litre _____
2 A booklet with six pages _____
3 A car with four doors _____
4 A bill for ten pounds _____
5 A race over five miles _____

**Book 6** 103